The
SPECIAL NEEDS
ACCEPTANCE
BOOK

Being a Friend to Someone with Special Needs

by Ellen Sabin

and _____

WRITE YOUR NAME HERE

WATERING CAN® PRESS

WATERING CAN®

Growing Kids with Character

When you care about things and nurture them,
they will grow healthy, strong, and happy, and in turn,
will make the world a better place.

Several website addresses (URLs) are provided in this book as resource references.
The publisher does not maintain these sites, all of which were active and valid
at the time of publication. Please note that over time, URLs and/or their content
may change. We regret any inconvenience this may cause readers.

Written by Ellen Sabin
Illustrated by Kerren Barbas
Designed by Heather Zschock

ISBN-13: 978-0-9759868-5-1
ISBN-10: 0-9759868-5-6
Printed in China

Website address: www.wateringcanpress.com

Dear _____,

Because you are such a nice, caring, and kind person, I am giving you this **SPECIAL NEEDS ACCEPTANCE BOOK**.

With this book, you will learn about some kinds of special needs and how they might affect people.

You will see that, like you, people with special needs have their own skills and challenges. And, just like you, they want to be accepted and understood.

People with special needs may not always act, move, or look the exact ways that you expect, but if you take the time to understand them, you will get to learn new things and make new friends.

You may be living with a special need, know someone who is, or meet someone in the future who has one. It is important to remember that we are all more alike than we are different, and that we all like to be treated with kindness and respect.

From, _____

Some "thank-yous"

- To my family—my best editors and critics. And to Heather, Kerren, Sam, and Josh; their talents and contributions show that a final product is only as good as the sum of its parts.

- There were many professionals who contributed their time, expertise, encouragement, and support. I especially want to thank Richard Robison, Dr. Mindy Aisen, Karen Margolis London, and Sharon Davis.

- I had the great benefit of speaking with many parents and teachers of children with special needs—each provided feedback that shaped this book and its message.

- Finally, a big "thank-you" to some very special kids! Their insight and input was invaluable.

A NOTE TO ADULTS

Children with special needs face many challenges. These children will have an easier time navigating the world if the people in their lives try to understand them.

Children who do not have a disability live in a world that is made up of people who are different from one another in all sorts of ways. The best way to teach children tolerance and acceptance is by encouraging them to take the time, and make the effort, to understand and respect others. That way, they will learn empathy and compassion and will learn to treat people in the ways they would like to be treated themselves.

When children learn about people with special needs they will be supporting their peers, making new friends, and ultimately strengthening their own character.

We hope this book will engage and inspire them.

It will give them an opportunity to explore and experience how it feels to be different, and how nice it feels to be understood and accepted. It will introduce them to the challenges faced by people with special needs.

This activity book will support their personal journey toward appreciating and respecting people's differences.

Table of Contents

● **What Is The SPECIAL NEEDS ACCEPTANCE BOOK?** . . . 6
  Here's How It Works…

● **Take a WALK in Someone Else's Shoes** 10
  How and Why to Accept Others

● **What Are SPECIAL NEEDS?** 18

● **YOU and Your FRIENDS with Special Needs** 32
  Understanding What Makes Them Different
  and Special and How You Can Be a Good Friend

● **GROUP Activities** 50

● **EXPRESS Yourself!** 56

● **Other Stuff** 60

What is The SPECIAL NEEDS ACCEPTANCE BOOK?

Welcome to Your **SPECIAL NEEDS ACCEPTANCE BOOK!**

What do all your friends, family, teachers, and the people
in your community have in common?

They are all different from one another!

Everyone is different in some ways, which is great,
because this is what makes us all unique and special.

When people seem different from you, the best thing to do is to try to
understand them and find out what is special about each of them.

The **SPECIAL NEEDS ACCEPTANCE BOOK** will help
you learn more about people who may seem different
from you because they have special needs.

- It will teach you about a few kinds of special needs and about some of the things that may be challenging for people with special needs.

- It will show you that we are all different and have our own challenges to face.

- It will help you understand why people with special needs may sometimes act or move differently than you do, or look different from you.

- It will help you imagine how things might feel for people with special needs.

- It will let you figure out ways to be understanding, accepting, and even helpful to people with special needs.

★ You will see that when you make an effort to understand people, you will find their special qualities. That means that anyone can become your friend if you take the time to understand him or her. When you do this, you will build all kinds of new and valuable friendships.

What are you waiting for? Turn the page and get started! •••⟶

How does The SPECIAL NEEDS ACCEPTANCE BOOK work?

First You think about how everyone is different from one another and how nice it feels when people accept and include one another.

Next You learn what "special needs" means. Then, you learn about different types of special needs.

Then You explore how and why your friends with special needs may act or move differently than you do, or look different from you. You can even try to imagine some of the things that are hard for them and how things might feel to them.

And Once you understand how your friends with special needs may feel, you can think about ways to be thoughtful and supportive of them.

Then You can even do things with your classmates and friends—like raise money to donate to research about a special need. You can also share what you've learned with others and show them how important it is to try to understand, accept, and include everyone.

REMEMBER: This is YOUR book. Along the way, you can keep a journal, write notes, and collect ideas about special needs, being a good friend, and accepting others.

Take a Walk in Someone Else's Shoes

How and Why to Accept Others

Everyone you know and everyone you will ever meet is special and different in some way. The world would be a boring place if people were all the same.

It's our differences that make us all unique and interesting.

When people look different from you or act differently than you do, the best thing to do is to try to understand and accept them. In other words, learn more about them, be kind to them, and include them in the things that you and your friends do together.

One great way to try to understand people who seem different from you is to "walk in their shoes."

What does it mean to walk in someone else's shoes?

It means you think about what it would feel like to be them.

- You think about the things that are hard for them and imagine what it would feel like if those things were hard for you, too.

- You think about the things they do and don't enjoy doing and imagine feeling the same way.

- You think about how people talk to them and treat them and imagine how it would feel if people acted in those ways toward you.

After you use your imagination to understand a little more about them and how they may feel, you can then treat them how you would want to be treated.

When you take time to understand people and walk in their shoes, you will be showing your kindness, learning about others, and being a good friend!

How are people different from one another?

Here are just a few ways that people can be different from one another:

LOOKS

People look different from one another in all sorts of ways: Some people are tall and others are shorter; some have dark skin and others have light skin; some have long hair and others are bald. You can probably think of many other ways that people look different from one another.

SKILLS

People have different skills and talents—things that they are really good at and that are easy for them to do well. Some people are good at spelling or science. Others might be great singers or good at sports. We all have things that we enjoy doing or that we do really well.

CHALLENGES

People also have different challenges—things that they find hard to do. Some of your classmates may find that learning math takes them longer than it takes their friends. Others might have a hard time riding a bike or playing soccer.

Sometimes these challenges can be small, and people can work hard to improve at the things they find difficult. Other times, these challenges can be bigger and harder to overcome.

FEARS

Everyone feels scared sometimes. Some people don't like the dark and sleep with a nightlight. Others get upset when they see a spider or hear loud noises. The things that scare one person can be different from the things that scare someone else.

PERSONALITY

Some people like to play with their friends all the time. Other people like being alone sometimes, or playing with just a few friends at a time. Some people love to talk and share lots of stories with their friends. Other people might be more shy or quiet.

But even though everyone is different, EVERYONE wants to be included, accepted, and liked!

How are you **DIFFERENT**?

Here, you get to think about ways that you feel different.

There are many things that I think are fun and that I am really good at doing. One of the things I'm really good at is ....

There are also some things that are hard for me to learn. Some of my friends are good at these things, and I wish I were, too. One thing that I think is hard is .... When I can't do that well, I sometimes feel ....

I know that everyone looks different from one another and this is how I think I look different—I am ....

I get scared of some things that might not make other people scared. One thing that sometimes makes me feel scared is ....

I notice that people act differently when they are upset. Some people like to be quiet and alone; others want to be around friends. Some people cry, and some people might get mad and yell. When I'm upset, I usually ....

How do **YOU** like to be treated?

Now, you can think about how you like people to treat you.

When I feel different, I hope that people will: (circle all that apply)

treat me nicely

lend a hand

be my friend

BE PATIENT

NOT LAUGH AT ME

help me feel better

You probably circled all of them!

That means that you hope others will take the time to understand you, be kind to you, and walk in your shoes!

How are people similar to one another?

One part of walking in someone else's shoes is remembering that everyone also has some things in common.

LOOKS

People share many similarities in how they look. Our faces have two eyes, a nose, and a mouth. Many people have the same eye color, hair color, or skin color. We look much more alike than we look different!

SKILLS/ CHALLENGES

Each and every person has some great skills—things they do well, things they can teach others, and things that are valuable. Every person also has things that they find hard to do. They may put extra effort into overcoming those challenges.

FEARS

People may fear different things, but everyone feels scared sometimes.

PERSONALITY

Everyone has personality traits that are great. Everyone likes to have friends. Everyone likes to feel valued and loved. You can probably think of a lot of other things that we all share in our personalities.

So you see...
even though people
are different
from one another,
they also share things
in common, too.

Now it's your turn to learn about people
who may seem different from you because
they have a special need.

You've just seen that everyone is different and that everyone has his or her own skills and challenges.

People who have special needs have extra challenges that may require extra medical care, therapy, teaching, or other kinds of help because a part of their brain or body works differently from other people.

These challenges can develop because of a medical condition or an injury to a person's body or brain. These conditions are called "special needs" or "disabilities."

There are many different kinds of special needs.

- There are people who need special medical care because a part of their **body** has been hurt and doesn't work perfectly all the time. These people may need special equipment—like crutches, wheelchairs, or glasses—or they may need medicine or extra attention from doctors because they get sick easily.

- Some people need special attention because a part of their **brain** works differently. People who have a brain that works differently may think or act differently. These people often get special care and attention to help them learn and play with other people.

- Other people have special needs when it comes to **learning**. They might get extra help from teachers and classroom aides. Some people who have learning challenges are just as smart as their friends. Other times, they might not be. But, either way, they learn things in different ways and they need to work much harder than other people to learn.

- Some people have extra emotional challenges—they get sad, upset, or distracted easily. They may become active and fidgety often. When they feel strong **emotions** that they can't control, it may seem like they are misbehaving. Their parents, counselors, or teachers may give them special help or medicine to help them deal with these challenges.

The next few pages will help you understand more about a few kinds of special needs, including: cerebral palsy, cystic fibrosis, blindness, deafness, asthma, autism, Down syndrome, learning disabilities like dyslexia, and ADHD.

One kind of special need is called cerebral palsy.

Some people call it CP for short.

People with cerebral palsy have had a brain injury. They were either born with their brain injury or their brain got hurt when they were very young.

The brain's job is to tell the body what to do and when to do it. Each part of the brain is in charge of a different part of the body or a different type of job. Depending on where someone's brain was hurt, they can have different challenges.

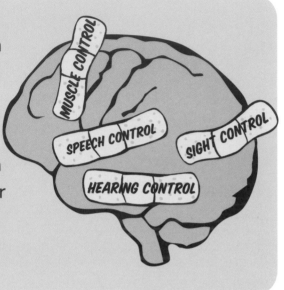

- If the part of the brain that controls the muscles gets hurt, then someone may not be able to use or control his or her muscles.
  - Since muscles control how people move, people with cerebral palsy may move in ways that make them look like they are shaking.
  - Sometimes people with cerebral palsy may lose their balance and fall.
  - They might use crutches or a wheelchair if their leg muscles don't work well. That means they can't play or run around like other kids.
  - They might not even be able to hold a pencil or hold up their heads.

- Sometimes the part of the brain that controls speech gets hurt. If that happens, people with cerebral palsy might have trouble talking or they might sound differently than you do when they talk.

- If the learning part of the brain gets hurt, then a person with cerebral palsy might have a hard time learning new things.

- Other parts of the brain that control hearing or seeing can also get hurt— so people with cerebral palsy might have extra problems with hearing or seeing.

Another kind of special need is called cystic fibrosis.

Cystic fibrosis is an illness that affects people's breathing and strength.

Here are some ways that cystic fibrosis can make things challenging for people who have it:

▶ It takes energy to run around, exercise, and play. What gives you energy? Food. People with cystic fibrosis don't get as much energy from their food as you do. As a result, they can get tired very easily. They might not be able to play sports or join other fun activities that require lots of strength and energy.

▶ When you get a cold, you might feel badly and need to stay home from school for a day or two. When your friends with cystic fibrosis get a cold, they may have difficulty breathing. An infection can make them a lot sicker than other people. They might need to go to the hospital if they catch your cold. So they have to be very careful to avoid getting sick.

▶ People with cystic fibrosis also get sick more often than other people do. That means that kids with cystic fibrosis probably miss a lot of school, so they might fall behind in class or miss lots of fun stuff with their friends.

People with cystic fibrosis mostly look and act like everyone else. But, as you see, they have extra challenges.

Even people who have challenges that you can't see still like to have extra understanding from their friends.

There are other special needs that you, or people you know, may have that can affect a body.

People who are blind need to learn to move around safely even though they can't see. In order to read, they may use special books with words that they can feel, called Braille. They may also use special computers, books on tape, or other new technologies to help them read and learn. They may have special dogs that guide them or show them safe ways to move around.

Some people can't hear at all—these people are called deaf. They may use sign language to communicate by using their hands. Other people may hear but just not as much as others. They may wear hearing aids to make sounds louder.

People with asthma have problems breathing. They may get tired and out of breath more easily than other people. People with asthma often need special medicine to help them breathe better.

You've just learned about several conditions that require people to get extra medical help or attention. Here are the names of some other conditions that you might want to learn about: muscular dystrophy, cancer, spina bifida, and diabetes.

People who have bodies that don't work perfectly all the time can't move around like everyone else.

Here's a way to imagine how that might feel, and to practice walking in someone else's shoes.

Write down the activities you do during recess, and also the people who you do them with.

Now, pretend you can't move your body to do those things anymore.
Would you feel left out? Would you want your friends to do different things with you now?

List the things that would be harder for you to do if you were in a wheelchair?

Now, make a list of things that might be difficult to do if you couldn't see:

I bet you understand a little more about how it might feel for people who have special needs that limit how their bodies move or work.

Autism is a condition that affects the way some people's brains work.

People with autism are "wired" differently from other people. This means that their brains work differently. As a result, they might not act or behave like everyone else all the time. They are not dumb or wrong, they are just different in some ways.

Here are some ways that people with autism may act differently:

- People with autism often find it very difficult to express how they are feeling or to talk. Some people with autism may not even be able to talk at all. It can also be challenging for people with autism to understand what other people are saying.

- When people with autism have toys, books, or other things around them, they may not seem interested in these things. They may not play with them or use them in the ways that other people might.

- People with autism often have a hard time making friends or learning how to act around other people.

So you see, some of the things that are easy for you to do— like talking, learning, playing, and making friends— are sometimes very hard for people with autism.

Down syndrome is another condition that affects how some people's brains work— and also how a person might look.

People with Down syndrome are born with a different makeup. They have an extra chromosome. Chromosomes are tiny parts of the body that control how every part of you grows and develops.

Here are some ways that Down syndrome can affect people:

Having an extra chromosome can make people with Down syndrome look different. They are often short. Their faces may look more flat than round, and their eyes may look slanted.

People with Down syndrome can sound different when they speak. That can happen for several reasons. Sometimes the shape of their mouths or the muscles they use to speak with are different, so their speech may not sound as clear.

People with Down syndrome often enjoy learning, but they may learn more slowly than other people. Sometimes people with Down syndrome can learn as much as their friends; other times they cannot.

They often have difficulty hearing, and they can have other physical challenges that can make them need extra medical care.

Just like everyone, people with Down syndrome have feelings. They don't like to be stared at if they look different. And just like you, they like having friends and being included.

Some people with special needs may have a problem
in the way their brains deal with the information
that they get from their senses.

People use their senses to experience the world. The five most
well-known senses are seeing, hearing, smelling, tasting, and touching.

All of us feel overwhelmed by our senses sometimes.
Think of yourself and your senses.

- A bright light can hurt your eyes. (Sight)
- A loud noise might surprise you and make you jump. (Sound)
- A really gross smell can make you feel sick. (Smell)
- Very spicy food can make your mouth burn. (Taste)
- When you have a bruise and someone bumps into you, it can really hurt. (Touch)

These things don't bother most people very much.
But some people with special needs feel their senses
so strongly that all the information they are getting
from their senses can become very distracting.

What senses are you most sensitive to?
Answer the questions on the next page to find out.

How do you feel when someone shines a flashlight in your eyes?

....

Can you think of other sights that bother you?

....

....

Can you list three noises that make you want to cover your ears?

1. ....

2. ....

3. ....

What is your least favorite smell? ....

What do you do when you smell it? ....

There are things that you probably find uncomfortable to touch because they feel too hot, cold, sharp, slimy, or rough. What are some things that you don't like to touch?

....

....

Is there a certain food that you never, ever want to eat? What is it?

....

....

Everyone has different answers to these questions, because everyone has different things that bother their senses.

Some people with special needs have many more things that bother them because they feel their senses much more strongly than you do! Just imagine if there were lots and lots of sights, sounds, smells, tastes, and touches that bothered you and made you feel uncomfortable every day.

Now, I bet you can understand how some people with special needs might feel overwhelmed a lot of the time.

A learning disability is something that makes it hard for some people to learn.

People with learning disabilities need to learn in different ways or at slower speeds than other people.

One common learning disability is called dyslexia. To people with dyslexia, numbers and words sometimes look backward or jumbled up. Dyslexia makes it difficult for people to read, spell, and do math.

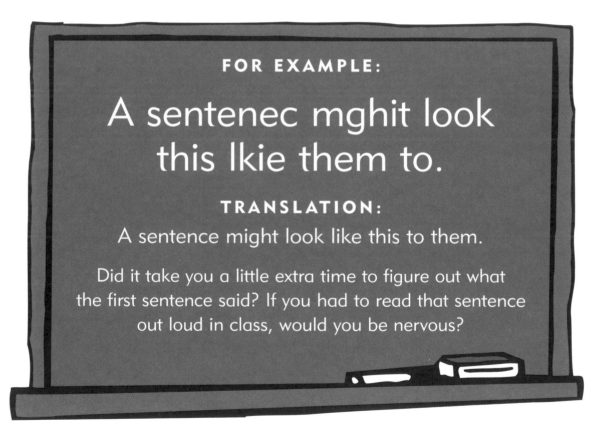

FOR EXAMPLE:

A sentenec mghit look this lkie them to.

TRANSLATION:

A sentence might look like this to them.

Did it take you a little extra time to figure out what the first sentence said? If you had to read that sentence out loud in class, would you be nervous?

People with dyslexia usually don't like to read out loud. They may worry that people will make fun of them if they don't read well. Many people with dyslexia overcome this challenge and do as well in school, work, and life as anyone else. They just learn in different ways.

Some people have emotional or behavioral challenges.

Some people have a hard time controlling their emotions.

They may become sad or angry or feel other emotions very strongly. Often, this happens when there are too many sounds and activities going on at the same time. Even when they want to stop and just feel calm, they can't.

They get help from parents and therapists, and sometimes medicine helps them feel better.

One kind of challenge is called attention deficit/hyperactivity disorder, or ADHD.

People who have ADHD can get bored very easily. They often feel overwhelmed by their senses. Sitting still and being quiet is really hard for them. That means that kids with ADHD sometimes run around or talk a lot. People with ADHD sometimes have tons of different thoughts at once and have a hard time concentrating on just one at a time. All of these thoughts can make them distracted or forgetful. ADHD can also make it hard for kids to sit still and listen to a whole lesson in class.

Some Common Things About Special Needs

You've just learned about some kinds of special needs and other types of challenges that require people to get extra help.

Here are some important things to remember:

▶ Some people with special needs have to spend a lot of extra time and energy working hard to do things that may come easily to you. Many of the things you do every day can be difficult for people with special needs.

▶ Special needs are not contagious—you cannot catch one in the same way you can get a cold or the flu. So, you don't have to worry about getting a special need by spending time with someone who has one.

▶ Sometimes you will notice a personal aide in your classroom who is there to help a friend who has a special need. These extra helpers are trained to understand your friend and to help him or her learn and to be a part of your class.

▶ Just like you and everyone you meet, people who have special needs can often do great things. Some people with special needs go on to become authors, athletes, doctors, and other things. They may also compete in sports contests, join scout groups, and graduate high school and college.

Many people in the world have some kind of special need. If you, someone in your family, or one of your friends has a special need, you shouldn't feel embarrassed. Just remember, everyone is different…and that's what makes us all special.

More About Special Needs—and how they are unique

In this book, we describe special needs and some of the things that people with special needs have in common. Remember, no two people in the world are exactly alike. Each person you meet who has a special need is as unique as you are.

- Sometimes it's easy to see when someone has a special need. For example, if someone is in a wheelchair, you can see right away that this person can't walk or run. Other times, it might not be as easy to tell. If someone has a learning challenge and can't read easily, you can't see that. Even so, the person still has extra challenges because a part of his or her brain or body works differently.

- Some people are born with their special needs. Other people had an illness or an accident as babies, or even as adults, that resulted in their special needs.

- Some kinds of special needs get more challenging over time. Other special needs stay the same, and people can learn to live with them for their whole lives. There are even some conditions that can become less challenging as people get older.

If you know someone with a special need and you become their friend, you will both be lucky to have that friendship. You will see that every friendship is different and has its own special value!

You and Your Friends with Special Needs

Understanding what makes them different and special and how you can be a good friend

Now, you will get to learn how and why your friends with special needs may sometimes act differently.

You can even try to imagine how they may feel. Here's your chance to practice taking a walk in someone else's shoes!

Remember, this means you use your imagination to think about how it feels to be like them.

Then, you can think about how you can be a good friend to each person you know.

Some people with special needs have very good hearing while some people with other kinds of special needs can have very little hearing.

Having great hearing may seem cool, because then you could hear all sorts of sounds that other people don't notice—like faraway cars, birds in the trees outside, or very soft noises. But for some people with special needs, having good hearing can mean that all of the different noises can get really LOUD and distracting and hurt their ears.

When this happens, they might cover their ears or wear earplugs. They might also talk to themselves so that the other noises they hear don't seem so loud.

Having less hearing can also be very hard. Some people may be able to hear a little, but they may not be able to hear a lot of what people are saying to them. Other times, people with less hearing can't hear at all. When people can't hear things that are going on around them, they may sometimes feel left out or alone.

When people can't hear well, they may ask others to speak louder or repeat themselves. They may also use sign language to communicate with their hands. Not everybody speaks sign language. This means that some people with less hearing can't always communicate with everyone like you can. Many people who have hearing challenges also might sound different when they speak.

Walk in their shoes.

How might it feel to have extra-good hearing? Think about the sound of a fire engine coming down the street, getting louder and louder and then stopping right in front of you. *How would you feel? Noises can be very upsetting, and when they are too loud, you just want them to stop!*

Here's a chance to imagine how it feels to have either no hearing or less hearing: Pretend that you are at school and everyone in class is speaking in a different made-up language. You don't understand that language, so you can't follow the lesson very well or answer the teacher's questions. Your classmates are talking and playing, but you can't figure out everything they are saying. You might even stop trying to play with your friends because it takes so much energy to try to understand what is going on. *How would you feel if this happened to you?*

Be a good friend.

When your friend seems upset about a noise, here are two things you can do: If you are making the loud noise, you can stop making it since you understand that it sounds SO much louder and might be hurting your friend's ears. You can also ask an adult for help if you notice that a noise is bothering your friend.

If your friend can't hear well, you can make sure to speak more loudly and clearly than usual. If you face him when you speak, he'll be able to see your mouth move, which can sometimes help him figure out what you are saying.

You can try to find ways to communicate that you will both understand. For example, you can use paper to write things down or you can use your hands to show what you are saying. You can even learn how to say a few words in sign language so you can communicate with your friend who cannot hear at all.

⭐ Some people with special needs do not like to be surprised—they feel much more comfortable when things are predictable.

Something is predictable when you know it's going to happen because it usually happens in a certain way or at a certain time.

Some of your friends with special needs like to have a schedule or a routine so they know what they are going to be doing every day. They do not like it when things change or surprise them.

If their schedule has to change or if they are surprised by something, they may get nervous, upset, or frustrated. Sometimes they will try to make themselves feel better by doing something over and over again. For example, they might work on a puzzle, clap their hands, or draw a picture. They may not want to stop doing this activity because repeating it makes them feel calmer. They also might go into a corner to be alone and quiet. Sometimes they might talk to themselves or make sounds to help themselves calm down.

Walk in their shoes.

All people have routines that they like—things that make them feel safe and comfortable. Maybe you like it when someone in your family says good night to you every night, and you get upset when that doesn't happen. Or, maybe every morning you go to school with the same person and it would be disappointing to you if that changed.

Write down some of the things that you like doing or seeing every day:

....

....

....

Now, think about how you would feel if these parts of your schedule changed.

Be a good friend.

Since your friend likes to follow routines, you can help her by reminding her about the day's schedule. For example, you might say to her, "In five minutes we'll finish recess and go back inside." That will help her begin to prepare for the change. Or, if something really new happens, like maybe a fire alarm goes off or an unexpected visitor comes to your classroom, you can be patient and understanding. Remember, these new events may be difficult or scary for your friend.

Some people with special needs may like to play in different ways than you do.

Some people with special needs can't always run or play sports like their friends. Maybe they have crutches, or their muscles aren't strong enough. Maybe their bodies move differently, so some games are hard for them. Some people with special needs can't always participate in sports because they might get sick if they get too tired.

Some people have special needs that affect the way they think and may have a difficult time using their imagination. They are much better at thinking about things that are real than about things that are pretend. Other people with special needs may have a hard time understanding exactly how to play certain games.

But, just like you, all of these people enjoy playing. They might be able to play your game if you make a few changes to it.

Your friends might prefer games with words and numbers, or they might like playing with puzzles or computers. Maybe they enjoy being part of a sports team—but instead of running around, they might like keeping score or taking photos.

Just like you, your friends with special needs like spending time with friends and being included.

Walk in their shoes.

Can you think of a game or a sport that a friend likes to play but you don't? Can you also think of a game that you find difficult or hard to understand? You might feel left out when your friends are playing games that you don't like or aren't good at.

Now, think about how much you appreciate it when other people agree to play games or do things that you enjoy.

Can you remember a time when someone made you happy by playing a game you wanted to play? Write about it here:

....

....

Be a good friend.

If your friend is not playing with anyone, maybe it's because he physically can't join in the game or because it doesn't make sense to him. If he's playing by himself, it might be nice if you tried his game with him for a while.

Maybe there are some ways that your friend can play a sport if you change the way the game is played. To give your friend a chance to have fun, too, try to think of safe and creative ways to let your friend join your games.

Sometimes, your friend might sit with you and play, but not talk to you. You should know that even if he doesn't say it, he appreciates and likes it when you spend time with him.

⭐ Some people with special needs might have a hard time talking.

People with certain kinds of special needs sometimes find it hard to talk or think of the right words to say. Some people may sound different when they speak or they may speak very slowly. Sometimes they might get stuck or confused in a conversation—they may forget what they are talking about or not be able to find the right word to say what they want.

Other people with special needs may not speak at all. They may stay quiet, hum, laugh, or scream. These people might learn how to communicate by using pictures instead of words, or they might use sign language or a computer to communicate with others.

When your friends can't find the words to express themselves, they may get frustrated. Knowing what you want to say but not being able to say it can be very upsetting. Other times, they may get very quiet, walk away from you, or make sounds. There are also some people who may just repeat back what you said instead of answering you.

Walk in their shoes.

Pretend you are in class and you can't talk. You have to go to the bathroom, but the rule is that you can't go unless you ask the teacher.

How would you ask the teacher without using words?

Would you point down the hall to where the bathroom is? Or draw a picture of a toilet on a piece of paper? Or try to pull the teacher toward the bathroom to show where you want to go?

If the teacher does not understand you or gets impatient with you, that would be pretty frustrating, wouldn't it?

Can you imagine how frustrating it would be to know what you want but to not be able to say it?

Be a good friend.

If your friend doesn't want to talk, don't be hurt, since you know that she just might be frustrated.

You can help your friend when she seems stuck in a conversation by suggesting some words for her to use. If your friend is repeating what you say, remember she is not teasing you—she is just stuck.

If her voice sounds different, be sure to never make fun of her. Remember, her voice sounds that way because some part of her body is working differently.

Sometimes, just letting your friend know that you want to understand her can be a huge comfort to her. If your friend is struggling to say something and is getting upset, you can tell her that you can see she wants to tell you something and that you will try to figure it out with her.

Some people with special needs look different from you.

Since some special needs change how bodies grow or move, some people who have a special need look different.

Some people are born looking different in some ways—their faces have special characteristics that are unique. Other people move their bodies around in different ways because they can't control their muscles very well.

People who look different or move differently still feel the same inside. They have feelings and they want to be treated like everyone else, even if they look different.

Walk in their shoes.

See the masks on the other page? Now, imagine if you wore one to school and didn't take it off for the whole day.

- Do you think that some people might look at you differently than they normally would?

- Do you think that some people might get scared of you, even if they knew it was you under the mask?

- Do you think some people might avoid you?

- Do you think some people might make fun of you and say mean things or tease you?

How would all of that make you feel?

_____

_____

_____

_____

_____

_____

_____

_____

Be a good friend.

Meeting people and making friends may be tough for your friend. Making an extra effort to be friendly and include her is a nice thing to do.

If you are meeting someone for the first time, maybe you can be the one to introduce yourself.

If someone is teasing her, you can stick up for her or tell a teacher.

If someone is making fun of your friend, you can remind him or her that everyone looks different in some ways.

⭐ Some people with special needs have a very hard time concentrating.

Some people get overloaded. They have lots of thoughts and ideas in their heads and they are aware of all the different sounds and sights around them. This can make concentrating in class and sitting still very hard.

Since it can feel overwhelming to think about lots of different things all at once, your friends may fidget, run around, and talk a lot. They might sometimes interrupt the class and forget to wait their turns. They may get frustrated and angry.

People who get overloaded like this don't mean to act in ways that disrupt other people.

They often try very hard to control their feelings, and they get help from special counselors or aides so that they can act more calmly and focus better.

$$26 + 34 = ?$$

$$3 \times ? = 12$$

To do:
1.
2.
3.
4.

Walk in their shoes.

Pretend you are in class and the teacher is giving a math lesson. All of a sudden, someone brings a TV into the room and turns on your favorite show. Then your best friend walks into the room to play with you, a radio starts to play a great song, AND it starts to snow outside. Just then, your teacher asks you to answer a math question.

Wow! You probably forgot to pay attention to her while so many other things were going on, right? Now, the whole class is looking at you and waiting for you to answer the teacher.

Now you know how it might feel to your friends
who feel overloaded and get distracted easily.

Be a good friend.

If your friend forgets to wait his turn, try to remember that he has a special challenge. Also, if he's not sharing, you can remind him to please take turns.

If he can't answer a question in class, try to be patient.

Teachers and other people might correct your friend often. It might be nice to take the time to give him an extra compliment once in a while.

Friends Value Friends!

You have seen that people with special needs have extra challenges that can make some things hard for them. But, just like everyone else, they have tons of things that are great about them!

My friend Alice is very special because she works really hard at things. Some things that are easy for other people are a lot harder for her, but she always keeps trying and that's really cool!

Susan can't see at all, but she can hear better than anyone I know. She knows all the lyrics and notes to my favorite song.

My friend knows a lot about trains, and I like it when he teaches me about them.

Steve is the best chess player in school. He says that since he can't play too many sports, he uses that time to learn chess. He wants to become the state chess champion.

John is very nice and patient. There was someone new in class and he was the first person to invite her to play with him.

Find the Positive

It's always best to look for the great qualities in your friends and in the new people who you meet. You will find so many wonderful things if you take the time to look for them.

If you know people with special needs, this is your chance to celebrate the great things about them that make them special to you.

What are some things that you admire and value about one of your friends who has a special need?

More Questions?

You've just learned how people with special needs may feel in certain situations. But you know that everyone is different, so each person who has a special need may feel and act different ways.

An important part of being a friend is learning all you can about your friends.

Here's your chance to learn even more about your friends.

If you know someone with a special need, you may have more questions. Maybe you wonder how he or she feels about some things or what he or she likes or dislikes. You can write down your questions here:

....

....

....

....

....

....

Here are some other questions that you might want the answers to:

- What games do you like to play?

- What makes you happy?

- What makes you sad?

- What are your favorite subjects in school?

- What can I do to be more helpful?

Now, ask an adult if you should ask these questions directly to your friend or if you should ask a teacher, your friend's parents, or someone else.

♥ A Final Thought About ♥ Being a Good Friend

Did you know that no two snowflakes are exactly alike?

❄

They are all beautiful and special.

❄

They are all unique and different in some ways.

❄

You and everyone you meet are like snowflakes—
beautiful, special, *and* unique and different.

The easiest way to be a good friend to someone
who seems different is to remember that—
like a snowflake—each one of us is special in
our own way and adds beauty to the world.

You and your friends can **LEARN** more about special needs and even do some things together to **HELP** people with special needs.

Here are some group activities:

Teach and Learn

If someone in your class or neighborhood has a special need, you probably want to learn even more about it. You and your friends can do research at the library or on the Internet. Then each of you can write a report about the things you learned and present it to your class.

Raise Money for Research

A wonderful way to show that you care about people with special needs is to help raise money so that doctors, scientists, and teachers can do more research about disabilities. You and your friends can make drawings and other crafts. Then, you can set up a stand to sell the art. Donate the money you earned to a charity for special needs.

Communicate Through Pictures

You have learned that some people with special needs sometimes have trouble talking. They sometimes might use pictures to express what they want to say.

Here's an exercise where you can practice communicating in a new way.

Each person should find a partner. Sit with your partner and, without talking, try to tell your partner what you did last weekend. You can draw pictures—you just can't use any words. Your partner should then tell you what he or she understood from looking at your pictures.

Each person should take a turn drawing to "tell" about their weekend while the other person tries to figure out what their partner is "saying."

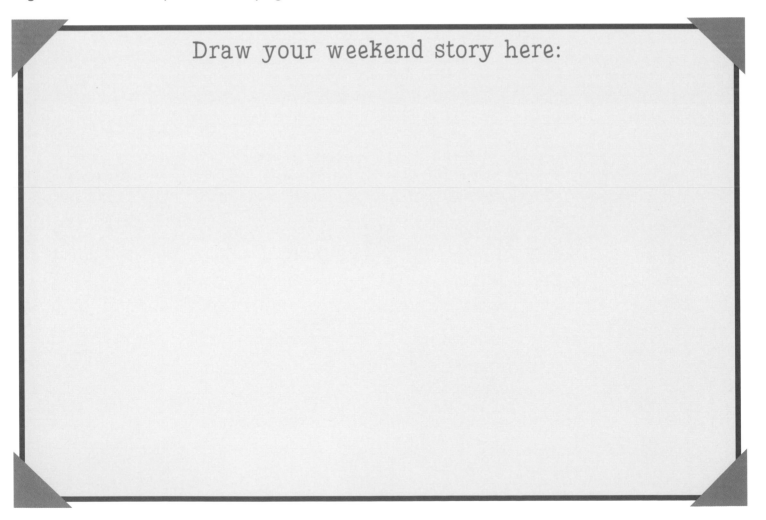

Draw your weekend story here:

Different is Special!

For this activity, everyone should sit in a circle. Each person should take a few minutes to think of something about themselves that is different and special. It can be a hobby, a talent, or anything else about them that is unique. Once everyone has thought of a special thing about themselves, it is time for the group to share their thoughts with one another.

One by one, each person in the group will explain what makes them different or special.

It's nice to see how we are all proud of the things that make us unique!

Compliment One Another

Now, since everyone likes hearing nice things from others, go around the circle one more time. This time, instead of telling the group something about yourself, give the person next to you a compliment about what makes him or her unique.

The compliment can be something specific, such as "I love your red hair," or "You are really good at math." It can also be more general, like "You always treat people nicely."

Doesn't it feel nice to know that the people around you like that you are different?

Learn About Some Special People

There are many people with special needs who have accomplished amazing things. Ask your parents, go to the library, or do research online about the people listed below. Then, teach your friends about your favorite special person.

 ## Helen Keller

What was her special need?

How was life challenging for her?

Was she brave? Did she work extra hard to learn? How?

What was a special thing that she accomplished that helped many other people?

 ## Franklin D. Roosevelt

What was his special need?

How was life challenging for him?

Was he limited by his special need?

What did he accomplish that made him famous?

 ## Ludwig van Beethoven

What was his special need?

What did he accomplish that made him well-known?

Do you admire him?

How was he special?

There are many other people who have special
needs who have done great things.

There are all different kinds of great things.

▶ Some people compete in sports even though their bodies don't work perfectly all the time.

▶ Many people succeed in school or at their jobs even though they had a really hard time in school because of a learning challenge.

▶ Some people are caring friends even though they have special needs that sometimes make it challenging for them to interact with others.

Do you know, or have you learned about, other interesting people with special needs? You can write about one of them below.

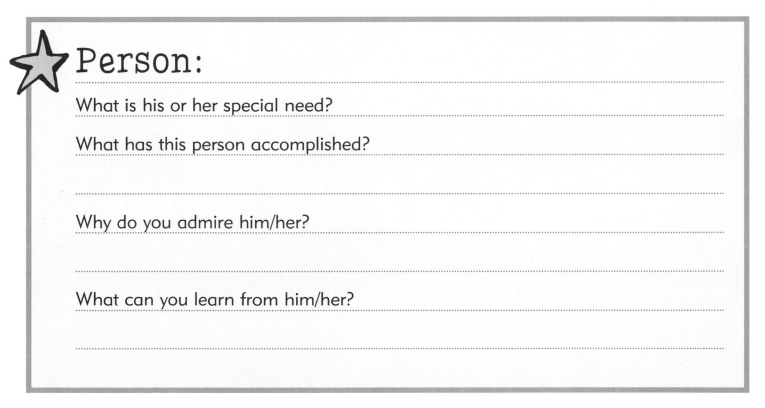

★ Person: ⋯⋯⋯⋯⋯⋯⋯⋯⋯⋯⋯⋯⋯⋯⋯⋯⋯⋯⋯

What is his or her special need? ⋯⋯⋯⋯⋯⋯⋯⋯⋯⋯⋯⋯⋯⋯⋯⋯⋯⋯

What has this person accomplished? ⋯⋯⋯

Why do you admire him/her? ⋯⋯⋯

What can you learn from him/her? ⋯⋯⋯

EXPRESS Yourself

The next couple of pages are blank for you to use how you'd like. You can:

Write a story about a time when a friend of yours included you when you were feeling left out or different.

Write a letter to the president or to your senator to ask him or her to support giving money to special needs research.

Describe how it feels to be around one of your friends who has a special need. Write about the ways your friend makes you happy or the special things about this friendship.

Congratulations!

You've learned a lot about special needs.
This SPECIAL NEEDS ACCEPTANCE BOOK certificate shows
that you take time to understand people and learn how they
are different and special. That makes you special, too!

THE SPECIAL NEEDS ACCEPTANCE BOOK

This certificate is awarded to

....
WRITE YOUR NAME HERE

for learning to walk in other people's shoes so
you can understand them and be a good friend.

....
DATE

Now it's your job to spread the word!
Tell your friends and family how important it is to try
to understand, accept, and include everyone.

Reference Ideas for Adults

There are many good sources of information for adults who are teaching children with special needs, for parents of children who have special needs, and for adults seeking to teach children how to be tolerant and accepting of others.

Some organizations that focus on special needs:

The Arc: www.thearc.org
Autism: www.autismspeaks.org
Cerebral Palsy: www.ucp.org & www.ucpresearch.org
Down syndrome: www.ndsccenter.org & www.ndss.org
www.rarediseases.org

Each of these organizations offers additional resources such as books, websites, support groups, and experts.

Other Resources:

The local PTA might have a special committee (called a SEPTA, or Special Education PTA) that has information for parents of children with special needs, including listings of specific resources in your area.

Parent Training and Information Centers and Community Parent Resource Centers in each state provide training and information to parents of children and youth with disabilities and to professionals who work with children. This assistance helps parents to participate more effectively with professionals in meeting the educational needs of children with disabilities.

The Technical Assistance Alliance supports these programs and offers many useful links and resources: **www.taalliance.org/centers/**

Join Watering Can Press in growing kids with character.

www.wateringcanpress.com

- See other Watering Can® series books.
- Order books for friends/family members or donate copies to an organization of your choice.
- Learn about bulk purchases for schools, stores, and organizations.
- View the FREE Teacher's Guides, and Parent's Guides available on our site.

We hope that you have
learned a lot about special needs and
the value of understanding people
who are different from you.